Our Journey

Abel García as told to Aurora Colón García

M000087248

Contents

Rigby

Chapter 1 Introducing My Family

Hola! That means "hello" in Spanish. My name is Abel, which sounds like "ah-BELL," and I'm ten years old. I speak two languages—Spanish and English—and love to play soccer. I'm also the proud son of **migrant workers** who plant, raise, **harvest,** and process crops. Migrant workers are people like my parents who move often to find work.

This is my family: *Mamá* and *Papá*—named Flora and Abel—and my four-year-old sister, Floranabely, whom we call Flora. Like Flora and me, my parents and their parents were all born in the United States. Most migrant workers are legal U.S. citizens. Before they were married, my parents traveled with their families from location to location in search of work in the fields.

Mamá, *Papá*, and Flora

Papá is a very proud man who has worked really hard to provide our family with our basic needs. He feels that to have a better life, it is important both to set goals and to work hard. As I tell you our story, you'll learn about *Papá's* goals. *Papá* comes from a family of 14 brothers. He and my uncles were all expected to work in the fields once they were old enough to pick crops.

It takes the work of many migrant workers to pick all the crops in a field. Because of them, people all over the country can enjoy fruits and vegetables at their dinner tables.

A mechanical picker can pick crops more quickly than a person can. However, it doesn't pick *all* of the crops in a field.

My parents, like many migrant workers, worry because machines called **mechanical pickers** are now doing much of the picking. A mechanical picker can do the work of 20 to 30 migrant workers. However, migrant workers are still the best workers because machines can only harvest about 90 percent of the crops in a field. Therefore, even though machines are being used, there is still plenty of work for my parents and other migrant workers.

5

Chapter 2

Preparing for Our Journey

My family has traveled to many places on our migrant journeys, and some of our stays were longer than just one harvest season. However, we have always come back home to Edinburg, Texas. It was always comforting to know that family, friends, and a home were waiting there for us.

On most of our migrant journeys, several relatives would join us. Sometimes it would be my aunts on *Mamá's* side or my uncles on *Papá's*, along with their families. Of course, there was one time when *Papá* got adventurous and our family went alone to Indiana.

My family lives in Edinburg, Texas. Between each of our journeys, we came back here to live.

Edinburg

6

I'll tell you about the last four years of my migrant journeys, beginning when I was six years old. My travels included Iowa, Indiana, Florida, and Texas.

We enjoy living in Edinburg with our many family members and friends.

Every time we prepared to leave on a journey, I was sad. I would be leaving some of my family and friends behind and going to a new place where I didn't know what to expect. *Mamá* would pack our bags with our clothes and other things that we would need for our journey. She allowed Flora and me to bring along one favorite toy. I always chose the same thing—my soccer ball—and Flora brought a small, brown stuffed animal.

Flora and I each got to bring one thing on our journey.

Then *Papá* would make sure that our car was safe for travel, and *Mamá* would prepare food for our journey. After that Flora and I would be buckled safely in the back seat of our car. Finally we were ready to take our place in the line of other family cars that were all going to follow each other on our journey.

Papá checked our car to make sure it was safe to drive across many states.

Year One: Harvesting Corn in Iowa

On our way to Hampton, Iowa, where my parents would work in the cornfields, we saw tall, green plants growing on land that seemed to stretch out for miles and miles. To me the weather in Iowa felt much colder than the weather in Texas.

At first it was difficult for our families to find work and a place to live in Hampton. We had to live without a lot of things, which was a challenge. Luckily, my cousin Carlos and his family were with us. Carlos and I were six years old and best friends.

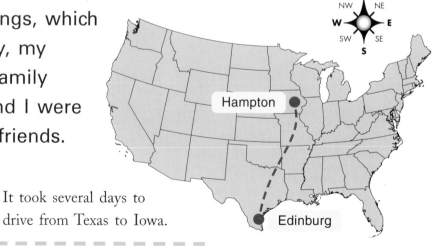

It took several days to drive from Texas to Iowa.

We crossed several states to get to Iowa. Along the way, we saw cornfields like the ones where *Mamá* and *Papá* were going to work.

Finally we found a place to live: a basement. It was scary because we had never been in one before. It felt good to have Carlos to talk to about my fears and to walk with me down those dark basement steps.

Going to school in Iowa was a challenge for Carlos and me. At home we spoke Spanish, but at school we spoke English. Fortunately we had a kind teacher who was very understanding.

Because Carlos and I had each other, school wasn't as lonely. Still, we were always relieved to go home where my aunt—Carlos's mother—would have glasses of chocolate milk and homemade cookies waiting for us.

Carlos and I liked coming home to this yummy snack.

When *Mamá* and *Papá* came home after an exhausting day in the cornfields, they had red faces, blistered hands, tired eyes, and muddy clothing. *Mamá* is only about five feet tall, so she is barely tall enough to remove the silk from a high corn stalk to mark it for harvesting.

We were all very glad when the corn harvest season was over, and we could go back to Texas!

It is very hard work to pick ears of corn off of tall stalks.

Chapter 4

Year Two: Canning Tomatoes in Indiana

The next year, *Papá* felt adventurous, and my family traveled by ourselves to Elwood, Indiana. There my parents would work in tomato fields. Tomatoes grow on vines that are shorter than corn stalks, so this work wouldn't be as hard for *Mamá*.

Elwood, Indiana, was surrounded by rivers and, like Iowa, had colder temperatures than Texas. However, it was just as green and beautiful as Hampton, Iowa. Luckily, housing in Elwood was not a problem for migrant families. We lived in **barracks,** or long houses that all looked the same.

It was colder in Indiana than in Texas, but the land was green and beautiful.

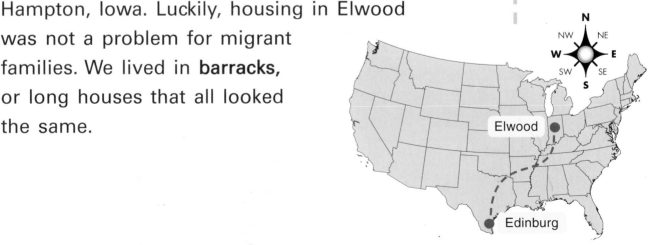

14

We were on our own because Carlos and his family—along with other family members—had decided to return to Iowa. School was a scary place for me because I'm very shy. I didn't make friends easily, even though there were other students in my classroom who spoke Spanish. I felt all alone and lost.

My family lived in barracks such as these. There we had plenty of space.

Then I met Abram at the barracks where we lived. He was seven years old—just like me—and even spoke Spanish. Abram loved to play soccer, and he was quick with his feet. He was from Pharr, Texas, which is very close to Edinburg.

My parents often came home with backaches from picking tomatoes off the vines. However, this never stopped *Papá* from playing his favorite sport with Abram and me. Everyone envied me because I had my own personal soccer coach!

Bending down to harvest all of the tomatoes from their vines is hard work.

Tomatoes and tomato sauces will keep fresh longer in cans than they will in the open air. Big moving belts help workers quickly put many tomatoes in cans.

When the weather was too cold to work out in the fields, *Mamá* stayed home while *Papá* worked in the tomato **canneries.** There they would put tomatoes in cans for many different kinds of sauces.

As time passed, *Papá* never forgot his goals. Therefore, he decided that the following year our next journey would be to La Belle, Florida. There we would live in warmer weather and stay with Carlos and his family, who were now living there. It was very exciting for me to see Carlos again. However, I knew that I would miss my new friend Abram.

We had to drive halfway across the country to get to Florida.

Edinburg

La Belle

La Belle—which means "the beautiful" in French—grows mostly **citrus fruits,** like oranges and grapefruits. As we traveled to La Belle, I saw rows of palm and oak trees. I also saw many different citrus **orchards,** or fields where fruit trees grow. The green leaves and bright orange and yellow fruits did make the land look beautiful. But even though La Belle was beautiful, it wasn't Texas!

Sweet citrus fruits grow on trees in fields in La Belle.

My parents worked in the orange orchards, climbing on ladders to pick fruit from the trees. Mechanical pickers were starting to be used in these orchards. However, the machines weren't able to pick all of the fruit off of the trees as the workers could.

Once again Carlos and I attended school together, but we weren't in the same classroom this time. We always looked forward to recess and lunchtime so that we could be together. Still, I did have a good time at school because there were other Spanish-speaking students in my class.

There were many nice places to live around La Belle, but I still missed Texas.

Carlos's family had bought a home in Florida because work was always available in orchards, fields, or **factories**. I was a little worried that *Papá* would like that idea and make La Belle our home, too.

My parents had to be careful when they climbed ladders to pick oranges. Luckily, there was work for them, even though mechanical pickers were also being used.

The migrant families we traveled with had common goals that bonded them together. We all worked very long days and faced challenges to make our goals a reality. In La Belle the migrant families seemed to settle in the same or nearby neighborhoods, so we shared many of the same experiences together.

We shared many fun activities with other migrant worker families during our journey.

The families in our migrant community often gathered together for special meals.

Our migrant community was closely united. We would get together for picnics and enjoy each other's company at gatherings in our homes. *Papá* taught us how to fish, and for a while we fished instead of playing soccer. In the summer months, we children felt safe because different migrant mothers took turns staying home from work to take care of us.

Chapter 6 — Year Four: Gathering Crops in the Río Grande Valley

Even though our year in Florida was passing quickly, I was still eager to return home to Texas. Then Grandma García in Texas got very ill, so our family *had* to return right away. While I wasn't happy that Grandma was sick, I was glad that we were going back to Texas because I missed my grandparents, my school, and my other friends. Even though I was having a good time with Carlos, I didn't want La Belle to be my real home.

Grandma García

24

The trip back to Texas was comfortable because one of our family goals had been achieved. We had gotten a big van, which had plenty of room for Flora and me.

Our new van makes traveling much easier. Getting it was one of *Papá's* goals.

The trip back to Texas felt like it took forever, but I was glad to be back home. Besides, I knew that we could always visit Carlos and his family back in La Belle with our new van.

Harvest begins in the Río Grande Valley in March and continues to the north through June and early July. Since all of *Papá's* goals had not been reached yet, he continued to work, picking seasonal crops.

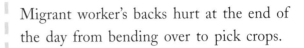

Migrant worker's backs hurt at the end of the day from bending over to pick crops.

We arrived in Texas just in time for him to harvest onions, cilantro, green peppers, melons, cucumbers, and spinach. All of these crops were close by, and he was lucky to be one of the workers picking them. Sometimes there isn't enough work for everyone.

Many of the fruits and vegetables that you and I eat are picked in the Río Grande Valley by migrant workers like *Papá*.

Chapter 7

Building Our Home in Edinburg

Grandma García was feeling better now, and we were safe at home. Meanwhile, Carlos and his family came to visit us. Another great surprise was that Abram's family had returned to Pharr, Texas. It was great to see them both. Abram is such a good friend!

The last surprise we received was that *Papá* was about to accomplish one of his greatest goals. *Papá* and ten of his brothers worked to design and build our beautiful new brick home! We are very proud of it. Since returning to Texas, *Papá* has worked in an oil field, as a mechanic, and now as a plumber. *Mamá* works at a Community Center helping Spanish-speaking families. Flora will be in kindergarten, and I will be in fifth grade this year.

I am very proud of my background because I know that families like mine—and the journeys that we take—play an important part in the lives of other people.

We are all proud that *Papá* has accomplished his goals.

Our Journey
(1997–2001)

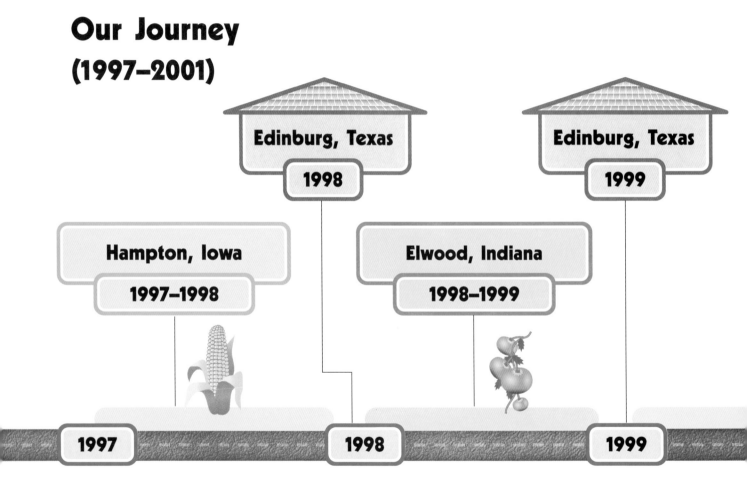

Edinburg, Texas
1998

Edinburg, Texas
1999

Hampton, Iowa
1997–1998

Elwood, Indiana
1998–1999

1997

1998

1999

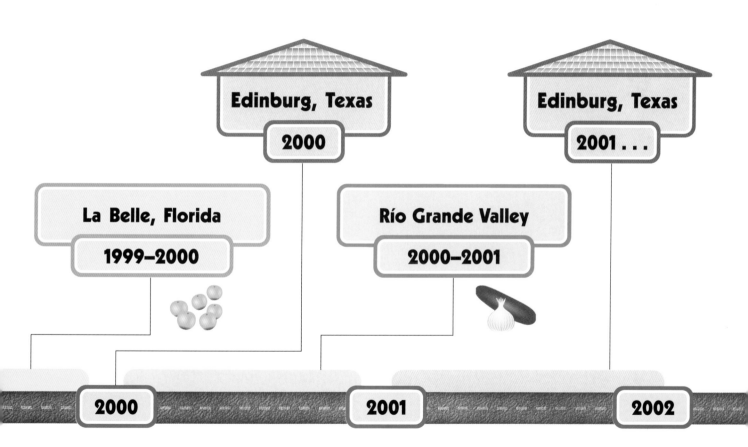

Edinburg, Texas
2000

Edinburg, Texas
2001 . . .

La Belle, Florida
1999–2000

Río Grande Valley
2000–2001

2000

2001

2002

Glossary

barracks a building where a group of people can live together

cannery a factory where food is put into cans

citrus fruit a fruit containing vitamin C, such as an orange, a lemon, or a grapefruit

factory a building where crops are processed and packaged

harvest to pick crops

mechanical picker a machine that can pick crops

migrant worker a person who travels to find work

orchard land where many fruit trees are grown together